"The Game-Changer: Instagram Influencer Marketing for Revenue Generation"

Introduction

In today's digital age, social media has become an essential part of our lives. It has revolutionized the way we interact with each other, consume content, and even shop for products. Among all the social media platforms, Instagram stands out as a game-changer, providing businesses with new opportunities to connect with customers and generate revenue. Instagram has over one billion monthly active users, and its visual nature makes it an ideal platform for influencer marketing.

Influencer marketing has emerged as a powerful tool for businesses to reach a wider audience and increase revenue. By partnering with influencers, businesses can leverage their massive followings to promote products and services to their engaged audiences. Influencers have become the modern-day celebrities, and their endorsements can sway the purchasing decisions of their followers.

This eBook aims to provide insights into the world of Instagram influencer marketing and its potential for revenue generation. We will explore the benefits of influencer marketing, the different types of influencers, how to find and partner with influencers, and best practices for a successful influencer marketing campaign. We will also share case studies of businesses that have successfully used Instagram influencer marketing to drive revenue growth.

Whether you are a small business owner, a marketer, or an entrepreneur, this eBook will provide you with the knowledge and tools to harness the power of Instagram influencer marketing and take your revenue generation to the next level.

Index

1. Increased brand awareness: Influencer marketing can increase brand awareness by exposing your products to a larger audience through an influencer's post.

2. Targeted reach: Influencers have a specific target audience that they have built through their content. Partnering with an influencer in your industry can help you reach that specific audience.

3. Cost-effective: Compared to traditional advertising, influencer marketing can be cost-effective, as you can partner with influencers who have a smaller following.

4. Trustworthy endorsements: Influencers have built trust with their followers, and their endorsement of your product can lead to increased sales.

5. Authenticity: Influencers are known for their authenticity, and their endorsement of your product can feel more genuine to their followers.

6. Increased engagement: Influencer posts can drive higher engagement rates, leading to increased visibility for your brand.

7. Social proof: Influencer marketing can provide social proof for your product, as followers may see others using it and become more inclined to purchase it.

8. Measurable results: You can track the success of your influencer marketing campaigns using metrics such as engagement rates, follower growth, and sales.

9. Word-of-mouth marketing: Influencer marketing can lead to word-of-mouth marketing, as followers may share their positive experiences with your product with their own followers

10. Enhanced SEO: Influencer marketing can help improve your website's search engine rankings through backlinks and social mentions.

11. Reach new markets: Partnering with influencers in different regions can help you reach new markets and expand your customer base.

12. Create compelling content: Influencers are skilled content creators, and their posts can help create compelling content for your brand.

13. Cross-promotion opportunities: Partnering with an influencer can lead to cross-promotion opportunities, as they may share your brand with their network.

14. Niche marketing: Influencers specialize in specific niches, making it easier for businesses to target their specific audience.

15. Stay competitive: As more businesses turn to influencer marketing, partnering with influencers can help you stay competitive in your industry.

Chapter 1

Increased brand awareness: Influencer marketing can increase brand awareness by exposing your products to a larger audience through an influencer's post.

In today's crowded marketplace, building brand awareness is essential for businesses to succeed. One of the most effective ways to increase brand awareness is through influencer marketing, which can expose your products to a larger audience through an influencer's post. This article will explore how influencer marketing can increase brand awareness and provide real-life examples of businesses that have successfully used this strategy.

Why is brand awareness important?

Brand awareness is crucial for businesses as it increases the likelihood of customers recognizing and choosing their products or services over those of their competitors. It can also create a sense of loyalty and trust, leading to increased sales and customer retention.

How can influencer marketing increase brand awareness?

Influencer marketing is a form of social media marketing that involves partnering with social media influencers to promote a product or service. Social media influencers have a large and engaged following on platforms such as Instagram, and their endorsements can have a significant impact on their followers' purchasing decisions.

By partnering with influencers who align with your brand and target audience, you can reach new customers who may not have otherwise discovered your products. Influencers can create content that showcases your brand and products, and their endorsement can build trust and credibility with their followers.

Real-life examples:

- Daniel Wellington

Daniel Wellington is a Swedish watch company that has used influencer marketing to increase brand awareness and sales. The company partnered with a range of Instagram influencers, including lifestyle bloggers and travel photographers, to showcase their watches in their posts.

One notable example is the partnership with Kendall Jenner, who has over 170 million followers on Instagram. Kendall posted a photo of herself wearing a Daniel Wellington watch, which generated over 3 million likes and increased brand awareness for the company.

- Glossier

Glossier is a beauty company that has built its brand through social media and influencer marketing. The company partners with micro-influencers, who have a smaller but highly engaged following, to showcase their products in their posts.

One example is the partnership with skincare influencer Caroline Hirons, who has over 500k followers on Instagram. Caroline posted a video of herself using Glossier's Milky Jelly Cleanser, which generated over 200k views and increased brand awareness for the company.

- Gymshark

Gymshark is a fitness apparel company that has used influencer marketing to become one of the fastest-growing companies in the UK. The company partners with fitness influencers, who showcase their products in their posts and stories.

One example is the partnership with fitness influencer Whitney Simmons, who has over 3 million followers on Instagram. Whitney posted a photo of herself wearing Gymshark leggings, which generated over 500k likes and increased brand awareness for the company.

- MVMT

MVMT is a watch and accessories company that has used influencer marketing to grow its brand and increase sales. The company partners with a range of influencers, including fashion bloggers and travel photographers, to showcase their products in their posts.

One notable example is the partnership with lifestyle influencer Danielle Bernstein, who has over 2 million followers on Instagram. Danielle posted a photo of herself wearing MVMT sunglasses, which generated over 100k likes and increased brand awareness for the company.

Conclusion:

Influencer marketing can be a highly effective strategy for increasing brand awareness and reaching a wider audience. By partnering with influencers who align with your brand and target audience, you can showcase your products to their engaged following, build trust and credibility, and ultimately increase sales and customer loyalty. The real-life examples of Daniel Wellington,

Glossier, Gymshark, and MVMT demonstrate the power of influencer marketing in building brand awareness and growing businesses.

Chapter 2

Targeted reach: Influencers have a specific target audience that they have built through their content. Partnering with an influencer in your industry can help you reach that specific audience.

Influencer marketing has become a popular marketing strategy for businesses looking to increase their reach and engage with their target audience. One of the key benefits of influencer marketing is the targeted reach it provides. Influencers have built a specific audience through their content, and partnering with an influencer in your industry can help you reach that specific audience. This article will explore how influencer marketing can provide targeted reach and provide real-life examples of businesses that have successfully used this strategy.

Why is targeted reach important?

Targeted reach is important for businesses as it allows them to reach a specific audience that is more likely to be interested in their products or services. This can lead to increased engagement, conversions, and ultimately, sales.

How can influencer marketing provide targeted reach?

Influencers have built a specific following through their content, and partnering with an influencer in your industry can help you reach that specific audience. By choosing an influencer who aligns with your brand and target audience, you can ensure that your message is reaching the right people.

Influencers can create content that showcases your brand and products to their engaged following, which can increase brand awareness and generate interest in your products or services. Their endorsement can also build trust and credibility with their followers, which can lead to increased conversions and sales.

Real-life examples:

- Huda Beauty

Huda Beauty is a cosmetics company that has used influencer marketing to reach a targeted audience and grow its brand. The company partnered with makeup artist and beauty influencer, Huda Kattan, who has over 47 million followers on Instagram, to promote its products.

Huda Kattan created content that showcased Huda Beauty's products and shared tutorials on how to use them. Her endorsement and content helped Huda Beauty reach a targeted audience of beauty enthusiasts, which led to increased brand awareness and sales.

- HelloFresh

HelloFresh is a meal delivery service that has used influencer marketing to reach a targeted audience of busy professionals and families. The company partnered with food and lifestyle influencers, such as Mindy Kaling and Molly Yeh, to promote its service.

These influencers created content that showcased HelloFresh's meals and shared their experiences using the service. Their endorsement helped HelloFresh reach a targeted audience of foodies and busy individuals who were looking for an easy and convenient meal solution.

- Airbnb

Airbnb is a vacation rental platform that has used influencer marketing to reach a targeted audience of travelers. The company partnered with travel influencers, such as Nicole Warne and Chiara Ferragni, to promote its platform.

These influencers created content that showcased their Airbnb stays and shared their experiences using the platform. Their endorsement helped Airbnb reach a targeted audience of travelers who were looking for unique and authentic travel experiences.

- Fitbit

Fitbit is a fitness tracker company that has used influencer marketing to reach a targeted audience of fitness enthusiasts. The company partnered with fitness influencers, such as Cassey Ho and Kaisa Keranen, to promote its products.

These influencers created content that showcased their Fitbit devices and shared their fitness journeys using the product. Their endorsement helped Fitbit reach a targeted audience of fitness enthusiasts who were looking for a reliable and effective fitness tracker.

Conclusion:

Influencer marketing can provide targeted reach and help businesses reach a specific audience that is more likely to be interested in their products or services. By partnering with an influencer who aligns with your brand and target audience, you can showcase your products to their engaged following and build trust and credibility with their followers. The real-life examples of Huda Beauty, HelloFresh, Airbnb, and Fitbit demonstrate the power of influencer marketing in providing targeted reach and growing businesses.

Chapter 3

Cost-effective: Compared to traditional advertising, influencer marketing can be cost-effective, as you can partner

with influencers who have a smaller following.

Influencer marketing has gained immense popularity in recent years as a powerful tool for businesses to reach their target audience and increase brand awareness. One of the key advantages of influencer marketing is that it can be cost-effective compared to traditional advertising methods. By partnering with influencers who have a smaller following, businesses can reach a specific and engaged audience at a lower cost. In this article, we will explore how influencer marketing can be cost-effective, provide real-life examples, and offer tips for businesses looking to implement this strategy.

Why is cost-effectiveness important?

Cost-effectiveness is essential for businesses looking to maximize their marketing budgets. By choosing cost-effective marketing strategies, businesses can increase their ROI and achieve their marketing goals without overspending.

How can influencer marketing be cost-effective?

Influencer marketing can be cost-effective in several ways. First, businesses can partner with influencers who have a smaller following, which can be more cost-effective than partnering with high-profile influencers with millions of followers. Second, businesses can negotiate rates with influencers based on their budget and the scope of the campaign. Third, businesses can repurpose influencer-generated content for other marketing channels, such as social media ads and email marketing, which can save time and money on content creation.

Real-life examples:

- Glossier

Glossier is a beauty brand that has successfully used influencer marketing to reach its target audience and increase sales. The company partnered with micro-influencers who had a smaller following but a highly engaged audience.

These micro-influencers created content that showcased Glossier's products and shared their personal experiences using the products. Their endorsement helped Glossier reach a specific and engaged audience, which led to increased brand awareness and sales.

Tip: *When choosing influencers, look for micro-influencers who have a highly engaged audience and align with your brand values.*

- MVMT

MVMT is a watch and accessories brand that has used influencer marketing to reach a younger audience and increase sales. The company partnered with Instagram influencers who had a smaller following but a highly engaged audience.

These influencers created content that showcased MVMT's products and shared their personal style using the products. Their endorsement helped MVMT reach a specific and engaged audience, which led to increased brand awareness and sales.

Tip: *Negotiate rates with influencers based on your budget and the scope of the campaign.*

- MVMT

E.l.f Cosmetics is a beauty brand that has used influencer marketing to reach a younger audience and increase sales

The company partnered with influencers who had a smaller following but a highly engaged audience.

These influencers created content that showcased e.l.f. Cosmetics products and shared their personal experiences using the products. Their endorsement helped e.l.f. Cosmetics reach a specific and engaged audience, which led to increased brand awareness and sales.

Tip: _Repurpose influencer-generated content for other marketing channels, such as social media ads and email marketing._

Conclusion:

Influencer marketing can be a cost-effective way for businesses to reach their target audience and increase brand awareness. By partnering with micro-influencers, negotiating rates, and repurposing influencer-generated content, businesses can achieve their marketing goals without overspending. The real-life examples of Glossier, MVMT, and e.l.f. Cosmetics demonstrate the power of influencer marketing in providing cost-effective solutions for businesses.

Chapter 4

Trustworthy endorsements: Influencers have built trust with their followers, and their endorsement of your product can lead to increased sales.

Influencer marketing has become a popular strategy for businesses to reach their target audience and increase brand awareness. One of the key advantages of influencer marketing is the ability to tap into the trust that influencers have built with their followers. When an influencer endorses a product, their followers are more likely to trust and purchase that product. In this article, we will explore how influencer marketing can lead to trustworthy endorsements, provide real-life examples, and offer tips for businesses looking to implement this strategy.

Why are trustworthy endorsements important?

Trustworthy endorsements are important because they can lead to increased sales. When an influencer endorses a product, their followers are more likely to trust and purchase that product. This can result in increased brand awareness, engagement, and sales for businesses.

How can influencer marketing lead to trustworthy endorsements?

Influencer marketing can lead to trustworthy endorsements in several ways. First, businesses can partner with influencers who align with their brand values and have a similar target audience. This can lead to a more natural and authentic endorsement of the product. Second, businesses can provide influencers with the product to try and share their honest opinion with their followers. Third, businesses can work with influencers who have a history of providing honest and trustworthy endorsements.

Real-life examples:

- Daniel Wellington

Daniel Wellington is a watch brand that has successfully used influencer marketing to reach its target audience and increase sales. The company partnered with influencers who had a similar target audience and aligned with the brand values of simplicity and elegance.

These influencers created content that showcased Daniel Wellington's products and shared their personal experiences using the products. Their endorsement helped Daniel Wellington reach a specific and engaged audience, which led to increased brand awareness and sales.

Tip: *Partner with influencers who align with your brand values and have a similar target audience.*

- Fabletics

Fabletics is a fitness apparel brand that has used influencer marketing to reach a younger audience and increase sales. The company partnered with influencers who were passionate about fitness and had a history of providing honest and trustworthy endorsements.

These influencers created content that showcased Fabletics' products and shared their personal experiences using the products. Their endorsement helped Fabletics reach a specific and engaged audience, which led to increased brand awareness and sales.

Tip: *Work with influencers who have a history of providing honest and trustworthy endorsements.*

- Nike

Nike is a sportswear brand that has used influencer marketing to reach its target audience and increase sales. The company partnered with athletes who were passionate about the brand and had a large following on social media.

These athletes created content that showcased Nike's products and shared their personal experiences using the products. Their endorsement helped Nike reach a specific and engaged audience, which led to increased brand awareness and sales.

Tip: _Provide influencers with the product to try and share their honest opinion with their followers._

Conclusion:

Influencer marketing can lead to trustworthy endorsements, which can result in increased brand awareness, engagement, and sales for businesses. By partnering with influencers who align with their brand values, providing influencers with the product to try, and working with influencers who have a history of providing honest and trustworthy endorsements, businesses can achieve their marketing goals. The real-life examples of Daniel Wellington, Fabletics, and Nike demonstrate the power of influencer marketing in providing trustworthy endorsements for businesses.

Chapter 5

Authenticity: Influencers are known for their authenticity, and their endorsement of your product can feel more genuine to their followers.

Influencer marketing has become a popular strategy for businesses to reach their target audience and increase brand awareness. One of the key advantages of influencer marketing is the ability to tap into the authenticity that influencers have built with their followers. When an influencer endorses a product, their followers are more likely to view it as a genuine recommendation rather than a paid advertisement. In this article, we will explore how influencer marketing can lead to authenticity, provide real-life examples, and offer tips for businesses looking to implement this strategy.

Why is authenticity important?

Authenticity is important because it can lead to increased trust and engagement with the audience. When an influencer shares a genuine and authentic experience with a product, their followers are more likely to trust and engage with that content. This can result in increased brand awareness, engagement, and sales for businesses.

How can influencer marketing lead to authenticity?

Influencer marketing can lead to authenticity in several ways. First, businesses can partner with influencers who have a similar target audience and align with the brand values. This can lead to a more natural and authentic endorsement of the product. Second, businesses can provide influencers with the freedom to create content that fits their brand and voice. Third, businesses can work with influencers who have a history of providing authentic and genuine content.

Real-life examples:

- Glossier

Glossier is a beauty brand that has successfully used influencer marketing to reach its target audience and increase sales. The company partnered with influencers who had a similar target audience and aligned with the brand values of natural beauty and simplicity.

These influencers created content that showcased Glossier's products and shared their personal experiences using the products. Their endorsement helped Glossier reach a specific and engaged audience, which led to increased brand awareness and sales. The content shared by influencers was authentic and genuine, which helped Glossier build a loyal following.

Tip: *Partner with influencers who align with your brand values and have a similar target audience.*

- Airbnb

Airbnb is a vacation rental platform that has used influencer marketing to reach a younger audience and increase bookings. The company partnered with influencers who had a history of creating authentic and genuine content.

These influencers created content that showcased their Airbnb experience and shared their personal experiences using the platform. Their endorsement helped Airbnb reach a specific and engaged audience, which led to increased brand awareness and bookings. The content shared by influencers was authentic and genuine, which helped Airbnb build a loyal following.

Tip: *Work with influencers who have a history of providing authentic and genuine content.*

- Patagonia

Patagonia is an outdoor clothing brand that has used influencer marketing to reach its target audience and increase sales. The company partnered with influencers who shared its passion for environmental activism and sustainability.

These influencers created content that showcased Patagonia's products and shared their personal experiences using the products. Their endorsement helped Patagonia reach a specific and engaged audience, which led to increased brand awareness and sales. The content shared by influencers was authentic and genuine, which helped Patagonia build a loyal following.

Tip: _Provide influencers with the freedom to create content that fits their brand and voice._

Conclusion:

Influencer marketing can lead to authenticity, which can result in increased trust, engagement, and sales for businesses. By partnering with influencers who align with their brand values and target audience, providing influencers with the freedom to create content that fits their brand and voice, and working with influencers who have a history of providing authentic and genuine content, businesses can achieve their marketing goals. The real-life examples of Glossier, Airbnb, and Patagonia demonstrate the power of influencer marketing in providing authentic endorsements for businesses.

Chapter 6

Increased engagement: Influencer posts can drive higher engagement rates, leading to increased visibility for your brand.

Influencer marketing has become a popular strategy for businesses to reach their target audience and increase engagement rates. One of the key advantages of influencer marketing is the ability to tap into the engagement that influencers have built with their followers. When an influencer posts about a product, their followers are more likely to engage with that content, which can lead to increased visibility for the brand. In this article, we will explore how influencer marketing can lead to increased engagement, provide real-life examples, and offer tips for businesses looking to implement this strategy.

Why is engagement important?

Engagement is important because it can lead to increased visibility and reach for the brand. When an influencer shares content about a product, their followers are more likely to engage with that content through likes, comments, and shares. This can result in increased visibility, reach, and sales for businesses.

How can influencer marketing lead to increased engagement?

Influencer marketing can lead to increased engagement in several ways. First, businesses can partner with influencers who have a highly engaged audience. This can lead to a higher engagement rate for the content shared about the product. Second, businesses can work with influencers who have a history of creating engaging and shareable content. Third, businesses can provide influencers with the freedom to create content that fits their brand and voice.

Real-life examples:

- Daniel Wellington

Daniel Wellington is a watch brand that has successfully used influencer marketing to increase engagement and sales. The company partnered with influencers who had a highly engaged audience on social media platforms such as Instagram.

These influencers created content that showcased Daniel Wellington's watches and shared their personal experiences using the products. Their endorsement helped Daniel Wellington reach a specific and engaged audience, which led to increased engagement rates and sales. The content shared by influencers was engaging and shareable, which helped Daniel Wellington build a loyal following.

Tip: _Partner with influencers who have a highly engaged audience._

- H&M

H&M is a fashion brand that has used influencer marketing to increase engagement and reach a younger audience. The company partnered with influencers who had a history of creating engaging and shareable content.

These influencers created content that showcased H&M's clothing and shared their personal experiences using the products. Their endorsement helped H&M reach a specific and engaged audience, which led to increased engagement rates and reach. The content shared by influencers was engaging and shareable, which helped H&M build a loyal following.

Tip: _Work with influencers who have a history of creating engaging and shareable content._

- Gymshark

Gymshark is a fitness apparel brand that has used influencer marketing to increase engagement and reach a specific audience. The company partnered with influencers who had a highly engaged audience in the fitness industry.

These influencers created content that showcased Gymshark's products and shared their personal experiences using the products. Their endorsement helped Gymshark reach a specific and engaged audience, which led to increased engagement rates and sales. The content shared by influencers was engaging and shareable, which helped Gymshark build a loyal following.

Tip: _Provide influencers with the freedom to create content that fits their brand and voice._

Conclusion:

Influencer marketing can lead to increased engagement, which can result in increased visibility, reach, and sales for businesses. By partnering with influencers who have a highly engaged audience, working with influencers who have a history of creating engaging and shareable content, and providing influencers with the freedom to create content that fits their brand and voice, businesses can achieve their marketing goals. The real-life examples of Daniel Wellington, H&M, and Gymshark demonstrate the power of influencer marketing in driving higher engagement rates for businesses.

Chapter 7

Social proof: Influencer marketing can provide social proof for your product, as followers may see others using it and become more inclined to purchase it.

Social proof is a psychological phenomenon where people tend to follow the actions of others, especially in uncertain situations. In influencer marketing, social proof can be incredibly powerful as followers see influencers using and endorsing a product, which can lead to increased sales. Here are some ways that influencer marketing can provide social proof for your product:

1. Product reviews: Influencers can review your product and share their honest opinions with their followers. This can provide social proof as followers trust the

influencer's judgement and may be more inclined to purchase the product.

2. User-generated content: When influencers share user-generated content featuring your product, it can show their followers that real people are using and enjoying the product, which can lead to increased trust and sales.

3. Testimonials: Influencers can provide testimonials for your product, sharing their personal experiences and why they love it. This can be a powerful form of social proof as followers may relate to the influencer's experience and be more likely to make a purchase.

4. Influencer product collections: When influencers curate collections of their favorite products, including yours, it can show their followers that they have tested and approved of the products. This can provide social proof and increase sales for your product.

One real-life example of social proof in influencer marketing is Glossier, a beauty brand that has leveraged influencer marketing to build a loyal following. Glossier partners with influencers to share their products with their followers and encourage user-generated content. The brand has also created a community called "Glossier Reps" where they work with micro-influencers to promote their products. This community has helped to build social proof for the brand, as followers see real people using and loving the products.

Tips for leveraging social proof in influencer marketing:

1. Choose the right influencers: Make sure you partner with influencers who align with your brand values and have an engaged following. Their endorsement of your product will carry more weight if their followers trust and value their opinion.

2. Encourage user-generated content: Provide incentives for users to share their experiences with your product, such as reposting their content or offering discounts. This can show potential customers that real people are using and enjoying your product.

3. Leverage customer reviews: Highlight positive customer reviews on your website and social media channels. This can provide social proof for your product and encourage others to make a purchase.

4. Share testimonials: Use influencer testimonials and reviews on your website and social media channels to show potential customers why they should choose your product.

5. Build a community: Create a community around your brand, encouraging customers to share their experiences and engage with your brand. This can help to build social proof and increase loyalty.

n conclusion, social proof is a powerful psychological phenomenon that can be leveraged in influencer marketing o increase sales and build trust with potential customers. By partnering with the right influencers, encouraging user-generated content, and highlighting positive reviews and testimonials, you can build social proof for your product an grow your brand.

Chapter 8

Measurable results: You can track the success of your influencer marketing campaigns using metrics such as engagement rates, follower growth, and sales.

One of the advantages of influencer marketing is the ability to measure the success of your campaigns. By tracking metrics such as engagement rates, follower growth, and sales, you can determine the effectiveness of your influencer partnerships and make data-driven decisions for future campaigns. Here are some ways that influencer marketing can provide measurable results:

1. Engagement rates: By tracking the engagement rates on influencer posts featuring your product, you can see how many people are interacting with the content. This can help you determine the effectiveness of your

influencer partnerships and identify areas for improvement.

2. Follower growth: When an influencer shares content featuring your product, it can lead to increased visibility and follower growth for your brand. By tracking the number of new followers you gain through influencer partnerships, you can see the impact of your campaigns on your social media presence.

3. Sales: One of the most tangible ways to measure the success of influencer marketing is through sales. By tracking the number of sales generated through influencer partnerships, you can determine the return on investment (ROI) of your campaigns.

4. Website traffic: If you include a link to your website in influencer posts, you can track the amount of traffic generated from those posts. This can help you determine the effectiveness of your call-to-action and the interest level of your audience.

5. One real-life example of measurable results in influencer marketing is Daniel Wellington, a watch brand that has built a successful business using influencer partnerships. The brand has collaborated with influencers across various industries and has leveraged their large following to drive sales. In one campaign, Daniel Wellington partnered with influencers to promote a discount code for their products. By tracking the sales generated through the

campaign, the brand was able to determine the ROI and make data-driven decisions for future campaigns.

6. Tips for measuring the success of your influencer marketing campaigns:

7. Set goals: Before launching an influencer campaign, set specific goals and metrics for success. This will help you determine what metrics to track and ensure that you are measuring the impact of your campaigns on your business goals.

8. Use tracking links: Use tracking links in influencer posts to track website traffic and sales generated from your campaigns. This can help you determine the ROI and make data-driven decisions for future campaigns.

9. Track engagement rates: Monitor the engagement rates on influencer posts featuring your product. This can help you identify the effectiveness of your partnerships and areas for improvement.

10. Analyze follower growth: Track the number of new followers gained through influencer partnerships. This can help you determine the impact of your campaigns on your social media presence and brand awareness.

11. Measure sales: Use tracking codes or links to track the number of sales generated through influencer partnerships. This can help you determine

the ROI and make data-driven decisions for future campaigns.

12.   In conclusion, measuring the success of influencer marketing campaigns is essential for making data-driven decisions and determining the ROI of your partnerships. By setting goals, tracking engagement rates, follower growth, website traffic, and sales, you can determine the effectiveness of your campaigns and identify areas for improvement. With the right tracking tools and metrics, you can leverage influencer marketing to drive measurable results for your business.

Chapter 9

Word-of-mouth marketing: Influencer marketing can lead to word-of-mouth marketing, as followers may share their positive experiences with your product with their own followers.

Word-of-mouth marketing is one of the most effective forms of advertising, as people tend to trust the opinions of those they know or follow on social media. Influencer marketing can facilitate this type of marketing by having influencers share their positive experiences with your product or service, which can then be passed along to their followers.

Real life examples of word-of-mouth marketing through influencer marketing can be seen in the beauty industry, where influencers often share their favorite products with their followers. For instance, beauty influencer James Charles has shared his love for the Tatcha Dewy Skin Cream, leading to increased sales for the brand. Similarly, influencer Jackie Aina's positive reviews of the Fenty Beauty line led to a boost in sales for the brand.

Another example can be seen in the food industry, where influencers may share their favorite restaurants or food products with their followers. For instance, food blogger and influencer Jessica in the Kitchen regularly shares her favorite vegan recipes with her followers, leading to increased interest in plant-based eating.

To maximize the potential for word-of-mouth marketing through influencer marketing, it's important to partner with influencers who have a strong and engaged following in your industry or niche. Additionally, providing influencers with a high-quality product or service and encouraging them to share their genuine experiences with their followers can help to create a sense of authenticity and trust.

Encouraging user-generated content, such as through a branded hashtag or challenge, can also help to increase word-of-mouth marketing through influencer marketing. This allows followers to see how others are using and enjoying your product, leading to increased interest and potential sales.

In addition to word-of-mouth marketing, influencer marketing can also lead to increased brand loyalty. By partnering with influencers who align with your brand values and messaging, you can attract followers who are more likely to become long-term customers.

For example, sustainable fashion brand Reformation has partnered with influencers such as Aimee Song and Camila Coelho, who share the brand's values of sustainability and ethical fashion. By doing so, they have attracted a loyal following of environmentally conscious consumers who are likely to continue supporting the brand in the long term.

Overall, word-of-mouth marketing through influencer marketing can be a powerful tool for increasing brand awareness and sales. By partnering with the right influencers, providing high-quality products or services, and encouraging user-generated content, you can create a sense of authenticity and trust that can lead to increased word-of-mouth marketing and brand loyalty.

Chapter 10

Enhanced SEO: Influencer marketing can help improve your website's search engine rankings through backlinks and social mentions.

In addition to the direct benefits of increased visibility and sales, influencer marketing can also have a positive impact on your website's search engine optimization (SEO). This is because influencers can provide valuable backlinks to your website, as well as social media mentions and shares.

Backlinks are links from external websites that direct users to your website. These links are important for SEO because they signal to search engines that your website is credible and authoritative. The more high-quality backlinks your website has, the higher it is likely to rank in search engine results pages.

When influencers share your content or products on their social media accounts, they may include a link to your website in their post or in their bio. This can provide valuable backlinks to your website, which can improve your search engine rankings. Additionally, social media shares and mentions can help to increase the visibility and credibility of your brand, which can also have a positive impact on SEO.

Real life examples of enhanced SEO through influencer marketing can be seen in the travel industry. Many travel bloggers and influencers have partnerships with hotels and tourism boards, and will often share their experiences with their followers on social media. These posts may include backlinks to the hotel or destination's website, which can help to boost their search engine rankings.

For instance, the Four Seasons Resort Bali at Sayan partnered with travel blogger and influencer Brooke Saward of World of Wanderlust to promote their luxury accommodations. As part of the partnership, Saward shared her experiences at the resort on her blog and social media channels, including backlinks to the resort's website. This helped to increase the visibility of the resort online and improve their search engine rankings.

To maximize the potential for enhanced SEO through influencer marketing, it's important to partner with influencers who have a strong online presence and a significant following in your industry or niche. Additionally, providing influencers with high-quality content or products that they are excited to share with their followers can help to increase the likelihood of backlinks and social media mentions.

It's also important to track the success of your influencer marketing campaigns in terms of SEO. Tools such as Google Analytics can help you to track traffic to your website and monitor changes in search engine rankings over time. By monitoring these metrics, you can determine which influencer partnerships are most effective at driving traffic and improving your search engine rankings.

In summary, influencer marketing can have a positive impact on your website's SEO through backlinks and social media mentions. By partnering with the right influencers and providing them with high-quality content or products, you can increase the likelihood of these valuable backlinks and mentions. Tracking the success of your campaigns in terms of SEO can help you to determine which partnerships are most effective at driving traffic and improving your search engine rankings.

Chapter 11

Reach new markets: Partnering with influencers in different regions can help you reach new markets and expand your customer base.

Influencer marketing is a powerful tool for businesses to reach new markets and expand their customer base. Partnering with influencers in different regions can help a brand tap into new audiences and demographics, ultimately leading to increased sales and revenue.

One real-life example of successful influencer marketing for expanding into new markets is the partnership between fashion retailer H&M and influencer and model Tamara Kalinic. Kalinic is based in London and has a large following in the UK and Europe. H&M partnered with her to promote their new collection to her audience, which includes a large number of young women interested in fashion.

Through Kalinic's promotion of H&M's collection, the brand was able to reach new markets and expand its customer base in the UK and Europe. Kalinic's followers were introduced to H&M's products and brand, and many of them became new customers. Additionally, Kalinic's promotion of the brand on her social media channels helped to improve H&M's online visibility and increase their social media following.

To successfully reach new markets through influencer marketing, it's important to partner with influencers who have a strong following in the desired region or demographic. These influencers can introduce your brand and products to a new audience, and their endorsement can help to build trust and credibility with that audience.

It's also important to consider cultural differences when partnering with influencers in different regions. Influencers can provide valuable insights into the cultural nuances of their audience and help to tailor your brand message and product offerings accordingly.

In addition to partnering with influencers in different regions, brands can also consider collaborating with influencers in different industries to reach new markets. For example, a beauty brand could partner with a fitness influencer to reach a new audience interested in health and wellness.

Overall, influencer marketing is a powerful tool for reaching new markets and expanding a brand's customer base. By partnering with influencers who have a strong following in the desired region or demographic, brands can introduce their products to new audiences and ultimately increase their sales and revenue.

Chapter 12

Create compelling content: Influencers are skilled content creators, and their posts can help create compelling content for your brand.

Influencers are known for their ability to create compelling content that engages their followers and encourages them to take action. By partnering with influencers, brands can tap into this skill and create compelling content that resonates with their target audience.

One real-life example of successful influencer marketing for creating compelling content is the partnership between cosmetics brand Glossier and influencer and artist Petra Collins. Collins created a series of illustrations for Glossier's new product launch, which were used in the brand's social media and marketing campaigns. Her unique artistic style and strong social media following helped to generate buzz around the launch and create engaging content that resonated with Glossier's target audience.

To create compelling content through influencer marketing, it's important to partner with influencers who have a strong aesthetic and creative vision that aligns with your brand's values and message. These influencers can help to bring your brand to life through their unique content and storytelling abilities.

It's also important to collaborate with influencers on the creative process and give them creative freedom to showcase your brand in a way that feels authentic and genuine to their followers. This can help to create more engaging and compelling content that resonates with the target audience.

Another example of successful influencer marketing for creating compelling content is the partnership between athletic wear brand Lululemon and yoga influencer Jessamyn Stanley. Stanley created a series of yoga tutorials and content for Lululemon's social media channels, showcasing the brand's products in a way that resonated with her followers and showcased her expertise in the field.

Through this partnership, Lululemon was able to create compelling content that highlighted the benefits of their products in a way that felt authentic and genuine to their target audience. The partnership also helped to increase Lululemon's social media following and improve their online visibility.

Overall, influencer marketing can be a powerful tool for creating compelling content that engages your target audience and drives sales. By partnering with influencers who have a strong aesthetic and creative vision that aligns with your brand's values and message, brands can tap into the influencer's content creation abilities and create content that resonates with their target audience.

It's important to collaborate with influencers on the creative process and give them creative freedom to showcase your brand in a way that feels authentic and genuine to their followers. This can help to create more engaging and compelling content that resonates with the target audience and ultimately drives sales and revenue for the brand.

In conclusion, partnering with influencers can be a highly effective way to create compelling content that engages your target audience and drives sales. By collaborating with influencers who have a strong aesthetic and creative vision, and giving them creative freedom to showcase your brand in a way that feels authentic and genuine, brands can tap into the influencer's content creation abilities and create content that resonates with their target audience.

Chapter 13

Cross-promotion opportunities: Partnering with an influencer can lead to cross-promotion opportunities, as

hey may share your brand with their network.

Cross-promotion opportunities can be a valuable result of influencer marketing. By partnering with an influencer, you have the opportunity to tap into their network and reach new potential customers. In turn, the influencer may also benefit from exposure to your brand and the possibility of new followers.

One example of successful cross-promotion through influencer marketing is the collaboration between beauty brand Glossier and fashion blogger Leandra Medine, also known as the Man Repeller. Glossier partnered with Medine to create a limited edition makeup kit that was sold exclusively on her website. Medine promoted the kit to her followers, while Glossier gained exposure to her fashion-focused audience.

Another example is the partnership between clothing brand Levi's and Instagram influencer Chiara Ferragni, who has a following of over 23 million. Ferragni promoted Levi's new collection on her Instagram account, tagging the brand and including a swipe-up link to purchase. The collaboration not only helped Levi's reach a larger audience but also gave Ferragni's followers access to exclusive products.

In addition to direct collaborations, cross-promotion opportunities can also arise through reposting or sharing content from each other's accounts. For example, fashion influencer Aimee Song reposted a photo from sustainable fashion brand Reformation on her Instagram account, tagging the brand and exposing her followers to their clothing line. Reformation also shared some of Song's photos on their account, promoting her content to their followers.

When considering cross-promotion opportunities, it's important to choose influencers who align with your brand and target audience. For example, if you're a sustainable fashion brand, partnering with an influencer who advocates for eco-friendly products can lead to more meaningful cross-promotion. It's also important to establish clear goals and expectations for the partnership, such as the number of posts or the type of content to be shared.

In addition to Instagram, cross-promotion opportunities can also arise through collaborations on other social media platforms such as YouTube or TikTok. For example, makeup brand Morphe collaborated with beauty YouTuber Jaclyn Hill to create a makeup palette that was promoted through her channel. The collaboration not only led to increased sales for Morphe but also helped Hill gain exposure to Morphe's existing audience.

Overall, cross-promotion opportunities can be a valuable result of influencer marketing, as they allow brands to tap into new networks and reach new potential customers. By choosing the right influencer and establishing clear goals and expectations, both brands and influencers can benefit from these collaborations.

Chapter 14

Niche marketing: Influencers specialize in specific niches, making it easier for businesses to target their specific audience.

INFLUENCER MARKETING

In today's highly competitive business environment, it's more important than ever to find ways to target your specific audience effectively. One way to achieve this is through niche marketing, and influencers can play a critical role in helping businesses achieve this goal. Influencers are known for their expertise and knowledge in specific niches, and partnering with them can help businesses reach their target audience more effectively.

Niche marketing is all about finding a specific target market and tailoring your marketing efforts to appeal to that market. This approach can be highly effective because it allows businesses to focus their efforts on a smaller group of people who are more likely to be interested in their products or services. By working with influencers who have built a following in a particular niche, businesses can tap into this highly targeted audience and reach them more effectively.

For example, if you're a business that sells organic baby food, partnering with an influencer who specializes in parenting and nutrition can be highly effective. The influencer has already built a following of people who are interested in these topics and are likely to be interested in your products. By partnering with the influencer, you can reach this highly targeted audience and increase your chances of converting them into customers.

Another example is fitness influencers who have built a following of people interested in health and fitness. If you're a business that sells workout gear, partnering with a fitness influencer can be an effective way to reach this highly targeted audience. The influencer has already built a following of people who are interested in fitness and are likely to be interested in your products.

One of the most significant benefits of niche marketing through influencer partnerships is the ability to reach an engaged and highly targeted audience. These audiences are often more engaged and passionate about their interests, making them more likely to engage with your brand and become loyal customers. By partnering with influencers who have built a following in a particular niche, businesses can tap into this highly engaged audience and build brand awareness more effectively.

In addition, working with influencers in specific niches can help businesses establish themselves as experts in those areas. By partnering with influencers who have already built a following in a particular niche, businesses can leverage their expertise and knowledge to build credibility and establish themselves as experts in that area. This can help build trust with potential customers and increase the likelihood of converting them into loyal customers.

For example, a beauty brand partnering with a makeup artist influencer who has built a following for their expertise in makeup and skincare can help the brand establish themselves as experts in the beauty industry. The influencer can create content and tutorials featuring the brand's products, showcasing how they can be used to achieve certain looks or address specific skincare concerns. This can help build credibility for the brand and increase the likelihood of customers trusting and buying their products.

In conclusion, niche marketing through influencer partnerships can be highly effective in reaching a highly targeted and engaged audience. By working with influencers who have already built a following in a particular niche, businesses can tap into this highly engaged audience and build brand awareness more effectively. In addition, partnering with influencers can help businesses establish themselves as experts in specific niches, building credibility and trust with potential customers. Ultimately, businesses that take advantage of niche marketing through influencer partnerships can gain a competitive advantage and increase their chances of success in their respective industries.

Chapter 15

Stay competitive: As more businesses turn to influencer marketing, partnering with influencers can help you stay competitive in your industry.

In today's highly competitive market, it's essential for businesses to stay relevant and find new ways to reach their target audience. One of the most effective ways to do this is through influencer marketing. Partnering with influencers can help businesses stay competitive and reach new heights of success.

Influencer marketing has become increasingly popular in recent years, with businesses of all sizes leveraging the power of social media influencers to reach their target audience. By partnering with influencers who have already built a loyal following, businesses can quickly and effectively promote their products or services to a highly engaged audience.

One example of a company that has successfully used influencer marketing to stay competitive is Glossier, a beauty brand that has grown rapidly over the past few years. Glossier has worked with a variety of influencers to promote its products, including beauty bloggers, fashion influencers, and lifestyle bloggers. By partnering with influencers who already have a dedicated following in the beauty industry, Glossier has been able to tap into a highly engaged audience and stay competitive in the crowded beauty market.

Tips for businesses looking to stay competitive through influencer marketing:

Identify the right influencers: It's essential to partner with influencers who are a good fit for your brand and have a following that matches your target audience. Conduct thorough research to find influencers who align with your brand's values and can help you reach the right audience.

Set clear goals: Before launching an influencer marketing campaign, it's important to define your goals and what you hope to achieve. This will help you measure the success of your campaign and make any necessary adjustments.

Create compelling content: Influencer marketing relies heavily on content creation, so it's essential to work with influencers who are skilled at creating engaging content. Collaborate with influencers to create content that aligns with your brand's values and resonates with your target audience.

Be transparent: It's important to be transparent with your audience about any influencer partnerships. This helps build trust with your audience and ensures that your marketing efforts are ethical and authentic.

Monitor and measure results: To stay competitive, it's important to monitor and measure the success of your influencer marketing campaigns. Use metrics such as engagement rates, follower growth, and sales to track your progress and make any necessary adjustments.

In conclusion, influencer marketing can be a game-changer for businesses looking to stay competitive in their industry. By partnering with influencers who have already built a loyal following, businesses can quickly and effectively reach their target audience and promote their products or services. To be successful with influencer marketing, it's important to identify the right influencers, set clear goals, create compelling content, be transparent, and monitor and measure results.

Thankyou.